T0209376

THE SECOND THING ABOUT GOD

Should Be the First Thing about Us

ELEEO ZAMZUMMIN

WESTBOW
P R E S S®
A DIVISION OF THOMAS NELSON
& ZONDERVAN

WestBow Press books may be ordered through booksellers or by contacting:

WestBow Press
A Division of Thomas Nelson & Zondervan
1663 Liberty Drive
Bloomington, IN 47403
www.westbowpress.com
1 (866) 928-1240

Scripture taken from the King James Version of the Bible.

ISBN: 978-1-9736-8607-1 (sc)
ISBN: 978-1-9736-8606-4 (e)

Library of Congress Control Number: 2020903037

Print information available on the last page.

WestBow Press rev. date: 02/17/2020

The Second Thing about God

Should Be the First Thing about Us

Eleeo Zamzummin

INTRODUCTION

From the fall of humanity until now, humankind has inflicted suffering on each other. I believe we are all guilty of that to some extent. It can range from slander, cutting someone off in traffic, theft, and lies to assault, murder, and horrific war crimes. We can watch on TV people lashing out at each other.

We can read in the Bible how God intervened in extended, out-of-control chaos with catastrophic might. If humanity is left to its own devices ... Well, as Jesus said, "And except those days should be shortened, there should no flesh be saved" (Matthew 24:22a).

God's heart is pained when He sees humankind hurt one another. We have lost track of who we were meant to be and who God is first and foremost. The greatest way God intervened was with the cross; there, He showed His heart, provided an example, and offered a solution.

Ever since humankind has stepped outside of its roles (caring for creation and fellowship with God) and has stepped into roles meant only for God, we have unjustly pronounced and executed judgment on each other. We have tried to be who God is instead of how God is, and we cannot do that righteously and justly because we are not God. We were created good—in the image of God. God wants us to get back to that. How can we do that and stop inflicting pain on each other? How can we get past ourselves, be aware of others' pain, and do something about it? How can we not be consumed by our pain and lash out in judgment, which only God is qualified to do?

I look at the biblical view of how we are to view suffering—ours and others'. I look at the failures of humankind and the church but never to beat them up; rather, I look at a problem that has a solution for those willing to change. Suffering will never go away until Jesus makes all things new, but can we cause less of it and lessen the suffering around us?

My turn to Christ began with the sorrow of realizing the suffering I had caused people who didn't deserve it, people I didn't know, people I knew and loved, and people I would never know. This happened while I was sitting in a prison cell as a young man. Since then, I looked hard for answers to why I had been so selfish, careless, and ignorant and caused others to suffer. This is what I found. I hope it helps you and others prevent and lessen some of the suffering in this world.

CHAPTER 1

THE FIRST THING ABOUT GOD

He stood on the mountaintop and called on the name of the Lord. Just days before, he had seen great power there. He had seen dark clouds covered the mountaintop, lightning, and black smoke rise to fill the sky as the Lord descended upon the mountain in fire. He heard thunder as the Lord spoke and a trumpet blasting from the mountaintop. Hundreds of thousands of people trembled below as they watched and felt the earth shake.

He had seen Egypt, the world superpower of his day, brought to its knees by epic plagues. He had seen a great pillar of fire stand between his people and the army of Egypt. He had stretched out his hand and watched the power of God divide the sea so that towering walls of water were on the left and right. He watched God hold the sea back until hundreds of thousands crossed to safety before it collapsed and drowned the army of Egypt.

But after having seen all these awesome things, Moses stood on the mountaintop wanting something else ... something even more awesome ... To see the glory of God. As Moses stood in a certain place atop Mount Sinai and called on the name of the Lord, the Lord descended in a cloud next to Moses. From the darkness of the cloud, the Lord picked up Moses and placed him in a cleft in the rock. The Lord covered him with His hand, and this happened.

> And the LORD passed by before him, and proclaimed, The LORD, The LORD God, merciful and gracious, longsuffering, and abundant in goodness and truth, Keeping mercy for thousands, forgiving iniquity and transgression and sin, and that will by no means clear [the guilty]; visiting the iniquity of the fathers upon the children, and upon the children's children, unto the third and to the fourth [generation]. (Exodus 34:6–7)

The day before, Moses had said to God, "I beseech thee, shew me thy glory" (Exodus 33:18). Seeing God's face would kill anyone (Exodus 33:20), so God protected Moses with His hand and let him see His back as He passed. (Exodus 33:21). The Lord showed Moses what he could handle without hurting him. Even seeing the glory from the Lord's back as He passed by was enough to leave the face of Moses glowing. God did a beautiful thing; He made all his goodness pass before Moses just as He had promised in Exodus 33:19. Even though Moses did not get to see God's face, God revealed His greater glory—His heart, character, and divine nature—to Moses in full detail as stated above in Exodus 34:6–7. This was the first recorded time God did that. From that point on, prophet after prophet would go back to this moment in Exodus and use it to point to God's heart as a plea for humankind to change their hearts. I am doing no different. I'm going back to this awesome moment when God revealed His heart to a man to start this book.

Why not call this book *The First Thing about God Should Be the First Thing about Us*? In Exodus 34:6–7, the first thing God said about Himself was, "THE LORD, THE LORD God" (Exodus 34:6a). So basically, the first thing about God is that He is God and being God is none of our business.

Playing God has been a big problem in the world and in Christendom throughout the ages. I am not talking about the occasional cult leader who says he is God (though I will say this line of thinking has its extreme result in such a declaration). I am talking about anyone in the church who is being controlling and judgmental outside of the scope of our role and authority permitted by scripture as Christians.

For an extreme example, throughout history, whatever group in Christendom was in power would often execute other Christians for things that were not even wrong. The point was not to keep people in line with scripture because more often than not, nowhere in scripture were the things they were killing for forbidden. The point was to be in power.

Keeping the Bible to themselves and speaking it in a language the people couldn't understand was another way of keeping power. How different is that from the day of Pentecost when the Holy Spirit enabled the believers to speak the truth of God in the languages of all who were there? Focusing on control, power, and judgment is not what God has called us to do.

God can make calls that we cannot; He has power that we do not have in terms of authority and ability. So it is very comforting that the very next thing God said about Himself in describing Himself, His heart, His divine nature, and His way was that He was merciful or as many other translations put it compassionate. He cares about the suffering of others as if He were suffering with them.

So why the great display of power to the Hebrews? Why the miracles in Egypt? Why the parting of the Red Sea? Why the awesome display on Mount Sinai with the fire, thunder, lightning, trumpets, and shaking earth? Well, two things. One, imagine if we had a compassionate but powerless god. Imagine he loved us and he meant well, but he had no power to provide for us, protect us, control the universe, and raise the dead. Well, such a god wouldn't be of much comfort, would he? God's display of power lets us know He has all the power, that power comes from Him as needed, and it is not something we need to grab for.

On the other hand, imagine if we had an all-powerful god but he did not care about our condition, our pain, or our future. Imagine if we had shaky hope. Imagine if he had the power to raise us up but doing so was based on our greatness, and even if we were to spend eternity with him, he wouldn't love us. You can see how comforting it is that God is all-powerful and has a heart full of compassion.

Yes, we were born into a fallen world. Yes, there is evil, pain, and death. But because God is compassionate, there is also healing, grace, comfort, forgiveness, a way for redemption, a promise of resurrection, and a plan to make all things new. His displays of power give us great comfort because His heart is one of great compassion and love for us.

The purpose of this book is not to go into great detail about God being God. It will not answer questions such as, Why did God do things the way He did? Why the fall? Why not make us like robots? and so on. God just simply stated the fact that He was God in Exodus 34:6a when He said, "THE LORD, THE LORD God," and there are many things we do not know or understand that only God, being God, does. But we do know the very next thing God said about Himself after that was that He was compassionate (Exodus 34:6a)—merciful.

We have all heard of or witnessed horrible things and felt pain and sorrow, and we may have asked why. We may have even questioned God's compassion. It keeps going back to the fact that God is God. He allows what He allows and does what He does.

After Moses asked to see God's glory, God said, "I will make all my goodness pass before thee, and I will proclaim the name of the LORD before thee; and will be gracious to whom I will be gracious, and will shew mercy on whom I will shew mercy" (Exodus 33:19).

Only God is God enough to make that call. Unfortunately, there were times in history when we were more concerned about playing God and grabbing power than showing compassion. As I mentioned earlier, being God is none of our business. God is the only one worthy of His position. I would like to bring to mind this scripture: "And after these things I heard a great voice of much people in heaven, saying, Alleluia; Salvation, and glory, and honor, and power, unto the Lord our God: For true and righteous [are] his judgments" (Revelation 19:1–2a).

Thank God that He is the only all-powerful One because He is the only One who can judge rightly 100 percent of the time. That is why He can say, "[I] will shew mercy on whom I will shew mercy" (Exodus 33:19b).

The first thing about God has to do with His position, and the second thing has to do with His nature. First on God's list of His divine nature is compassion, and we are participants with His divine nature according to 2 Peter 1:4. We are welcome to be participants with God's divine nature; in fact, we are commanded to be compassionate: "And be ye kind one to another, tender-hearted, forgiving one another, even as God for Christ's sake hath forgiven you" (Ephesians 4:32). Tender-hearted is translated as "compassionate" in some versions. Hard-hearted people do not show compassion. They do not let the pain of others penetrate their hearts because they are too consumed with the pain in their own hearts.

Philippians 2:1 brings out another aspect of compassion: "If [there be] therefore any consolation in Christ, if any comfort of love, if any fellowship of the Spirit, if any bowels and mercies" (Philippians 2:1). Bowels and mercies are translated as "compassion" in some versions.

Colossians 3:12 reads, "Put on therefore, as the elect of God, holy and beloved, bowels of mercies, kindness, humbleness of mind, meekness, longsuffering." Even though the term *bowels of mercy* is archaic, it brings out the deepness of the idea of compassion. You will not find a shallow person (one consumed with petty things) being a good example of compassion. In my youth, I was hard-hearted and shallow. After making a plea for us to be compassionate in Philippians 2:1, Paul argued that though Jesus was equal with God, He did not grasp for it. He showed us how important it was to humble ourselves under God's power and authority and not get caught up in these petty power struggles with each other. He made clear we were not to see ourselves as more important than others.

Having power for the sake of having power is very petty, especially when no objective follows that does anyone any good. Sometimes, I wonder if the pursuit of power is the pursuit of safety. However, it seems that the shell around one's heart gets harder and harder in this pursuit and the suffering of others increases.

Satan made the first power grab, and it didn't work out well. Then he got us to make a power grab in Genesis 3:5b: "Ye shall be as gods." The problem was it was "as gods" in God's position, in God's role, in what was only for God, not like God in His character. Satan tried to take God's position at the beginning (Isaiah 14:13–14), and he will try it again at the end (2 Thessalonians 2:4).

It is amazing how so many want to play God in His power and position but totally dismiss His character. The two things that bring one to that place—pride and fear—keep us from becoming compassionate. Pride is a pitfall that prevents us from being compassionate. We live in fear of losing whatever little power we grab for the sake of being prideful. King Herod for example was too prideful to bow before the true King and so afraid of losing his power (to a baby at that) that he murdered the babies in Bethlehem.

Unfortunately, position and power, the "I'm better than you are" and the "Me first" syndromes seem to be part of the fallen human condition. I'm sure we have all seen it pop up in ourselves. We can read about it in the Gospels when the disciples and some of their mothers even jockeyed for position in the kingdom of God. We read about it in 2 Corinthians 11:5 when Paul referred to false apostles who loved to put him down and elevate themselves in position and power. We can hear warnings from Peter when he warned shepherds about an attitude of "being lords" over the flock (1 Peter 5:3). We can hear John's rebuke in 3 John about Diotrephes, a guy who just seemed to like to be number one (v. 9).

How many times have drivers sped up to cut in front of you when they could have easily and safely dropped in behind you? If we Christians focused on living according to God's nature, just think how different our history would be and how different our effectiveness in the world would be. What gripped our hearts? Was it not the compassion of Christ? How then can other hearts be gripped if we are any different?

Interestingly, compassion often comes from a position of power or having the upper hand. Some give to the one who lacks. Some who are healthy help those who are sick, and some of the strong protect the weak. Some in authority are compassionate to those facing sentencing. Some creditors are kind to their debtors. Some who have the right of way yield it readily. The innocent can have compassion for the guilty. Some who can do so help the helpless. We can look at power or position not as something to be grasped but something to be used to show compassion, that shows people the heart of God, the most powerful yet the most compassionate of all.

To the Jews, Exodus 34:6–7 contains the thirteen attributes of mercy. There are different camps of Jewish thought on just how to break it down, but many Jews look at even the first Lord (YHVH) in Exodus 34:6 as compassionate to people before they sin and the second Lord as compassionate to people after they sin. Then El (God) is as mighty in compassion to give all living creation what they need. It is interesting that the Hebrews place compassion with even the greatest authority, God's name, three times, and then on top of that, the first word God used to describe the God He is was compassionate.

So the greatest position and title there is, that of being God, is merged with compassion. I wish I could say that the church was always compassionate. I can say that about Jesus. I can say that about the apostles, but I struggle to find the church having compassion as a dominant theme after that.

It seems that power, control, and condemnation were the focus in our history. It seems that after the church grew in numbers and had gained some worldly power, the focus was on keeping that power with ignorance, force, fear of condemnation, or just plain old fear. Even today, the last thing some would call the church and its leaders is compassionate. Some seem a bit more like Pharaoh, controlling and hard-hearted. That was the vibe I got as a child and even as an adult sometimes. Thank God for those compassionate unsung heroes we often don't hear about. You may remember a very compassionate church growing up, thank God. And thank God we have come a long way from the Dark Ages in most respects. Today, we can find compassion in many churches glory to God.

Let me go a step further where it hurts me a little. What would be the first word I would use to describe myself? There is a problem if it isn't *compassion*. I can think of a few words that best go right after my name at times that are not flattering at all. So yes, there is a problem. Fortunately, compassion is the best way to start to solve a problem. Thank God that compassion is something God is full of so He can have compassion on a guy like me who cannot say, "A hundred percent compassionate; that's my chief attribute." That's the direction I want to go because the first thing used to describe God's character should be the first thing I strive for to describe my character. Thank God we can grow.

Many times as a young Christian, I confused zeal with power and judgment. I believe that sometimes an unbalanced power and judgment mode may be due to an unhealthy focus in teachings over the years, a loner with a lack of good balanced teaching, or plain old ugly ego and sin nature making a power grab. Whatever the case, it's easy to fall into, but not at all what the Bible teaches. I often see older, mature Christians becoming more compassionate.

This book, however, is not about my having arrived, because I haven't. I wish I could have said, "Wow! I just found out that God is so big on compassion, and that's so cool because I happen to be so compassionate myself!" I couldn't come close to saying that. So when I talk about the failures of some of those in the church past and present; I am putting myself at the forefront. I am ashamed that my attitude toward those who got it right, who have God's outlook, has been one of "Yeah, that's great. I'm glad someone's doing it" if I even noticed them at all.

One reason I wrote this book was that I had failed for most of my life to have this outlook, and as a result, I have been the cause of others' suffering directly and indirectly. This book is about the compassionate nature of God. I hope it will inspire my readers to hope *compassionate* is a word they can put right after their names as their chief attribute. I believe that with this outlook, we will cause less suffering for ourselves and others and be compassionate and mindful enough to comfort the suffering of those God puts in our lives.

CHAPTER 2

THE LAST THING ABOUT GOD

> And the LORD passed by before him, and
> proclaimed, The LORD, The LORD God, merciful
> and gracious, longsuffering, and abundant in
> goodness and truth, Keeping mercy for thousands,
> forgiving iniquity and transgression and sin, and
> that will by no means clear [the guilty]; visiting the
> iniquity of the fathers upon the children, and upon
> the children's children, unto the third and to the
> fourth [generation]. (Exodus 34:6–7)

God said He would pass the iniquity of someone down to his fourth generation. I touch on this because this is in most cases none of our business and because some people talk about judgment as if it were the first and only thing about God. Remember that we are told to preach the good news. The world is already in the bad news. If someone lives in a ramshackle house ready to fall into the sea, we can go on and on about the house or we can say "Get out! Get in the chopper!" We can go on and on about all the sinking sand, or we can just point to the solid Rock where Jesus is extending His hand to us.

I've listened to sermons about how bad the world is without a word on what to do about it. It's usually the people who play God who love to go right to the last thing about God. While it is true that God uses nations and authorities to punish other nations and people who have gone too far, that's the last thing God wants to do.

Yes, the Bible is full of examples of God using nations, nature, disease, good kings, bad kings, prophets, or even supernatural power to punish. That, however, is not our call; it's God's call and a last resort. Sure, a parent can discipline a child, a police officer can arrest someone who breaks the law, a judge can sentence someone to prison, and so on, but it is not our business to decide when and how to punish outside the scope of our authority. It is our commission to preach the good news and have God's character, not to be some sort of monster of death. I am not at all saying we should deny the condition of the world or hell; I'm saying that an unbalanced focus on fear and darkness can cause us to neglect the whole point of living in God's light and love.

We sometimes forget how patient God is. God has sent prophets with warnings and poured out kindness for years. Sometimes, He pleads for hundreds of years for people to change their warped, sinful ways before He hands down a harsh judgment while we give others five minutes to change their ways.

God is so patient that it appeared at times that people or nations were getting away with the evil they did; God's people were pleading with Him to do something about that. Maybe that's the problem. We get so impatient that we jump right to judgment before God does. In 2 Peter, we read about those who mocked God's coming judgment because it was so slow in coming. Peter reminded them that God was patient and gave more time to people to repent because He didn't want them to perish.

Romans 2:4 says that it was God's kindness that led us to repentance. The context of 2:4—verses 1–3—was saying people were being quick to judge while forgetting the kindness God had on them. Paul was saying that we didn't have the right to be impatient with anyone when God was so patient with us. Jesus reminded us, "He is kind unto the unthankful and [to] the evil" (Luke 6:35b).

I'm talking about the danger of a reckless, unbalanced view

that right away skips to the judgment of God without a true picture of God's whole heart. I'm talking about forbidden judgment and punishment in the same context as Jesus did when He said, "Judge not, that ye be not judged" (Matthew 7:1). In the following verses, Jesus said that our judgment would just come back on us and how silly we would look pointing at a splinter in someone else's eye when we had planks in our eyes (Matthew 7:2–5). That plank just might be pride. We should be humble, see our sins as greater than those of others, ask God to remove them, and only then compassionately help others to remove what is causing them to suffer. No one likes splinters in his or her eyes—painful! But that's how sin is—painful!

Hebrews 5:2 is about a high priest who was being chosen: "Who can have compassion on the ignorant, and on them that are out of the way; for that he himself also is compassed with infirmity." We should be compassionate because we know that pain too.

Peter listed all the things in 2 Peter 1 that were God's divine nature for us to participate in. The list builds to an ultimate peak of kindness and love. Then Peter said that if we lacked these things, it was because we had forgotten how God forgave our sins: "But he that lacketh these things is blind, and cannot see afar off, and hath forgotten that he was purged from his old sins" (2 Peter 1:9). When we get proud of how we are doing as Christians and forget how sinful we were and sometimes still are, we stop being humble ... kind ... compassionate ... loving. The only reason there is a change in our lives is that we can participate in God's divine nature through Christ in us.

When people attempt to operate in the two forbidden areas—the first thing about God being God and the last thing about God—judgment—they often forget about all the great things about God in the middle that they are to operate in such as compassion, patience, kindness, and forgiveness. Instead, people in the power and judgment mode put all the stuff in the middle they are told not to have such as anger, malice, bitterness, unforgiveness, and envy.

A brief example is that of the older brother of the Prodigal

Son in Luke 15. Instead of being compassionate as his father was to his younger brother and rejoicing at his return, he was angry, unforgiving, and jealous. He would not come in and join them. He thought he himself deserved a party, not his brother. He sat in the seat of judgment rather than the seat of mercy. He could not be happy about the compassion his father showed to someone he judged unworthy though his father reminded him that his compassion had always been there for him too.

Jonah was a perfect example of this. When a prophet was sent by God to pronounce judgment on a person or people, the idea was to get them to change their ways. Sometimes in His patience, God sent different prophets multiple times especially to Israel and Judah.

> Yet the LORD testified against Israel, and against Judah, by all the prophets, [and by] all the seers, saying, Turn ye from your evil ways, and keep my commandments [and] my statutes, according to all the law which I commanded your fathers, and which I sent to you by my servants the prophets. (2 Kings 17:13)

God sent them all—every prophet and seer He had to Israel and Judah! So Jonah of all people should have understood that God, having compassion, would reach out to give someone mercy because He had done exactly that many times to Israel and Judah.

Jonah was sent to Nineveh and said it would be overthrown in forty days. Jonah was hoping this would happen, but God wasn't. They were the enemies of Israel. Jonah wanted to watch them be destroyed; he found a spot a ways off to watch the fireworks. However, these pagans believed God, humbled themselves, and fasted and mourned. So God did what He wanted to do; He had compassion on them and relented. Wow! And on their first prophet. God didn't even need to send them two.

Jonah was being taught a lesson in compassion. His head was

burning up from the heat, but a vine grew and kept him cool. Then God made a worm nibble at the root so it withered. The sun began to beat down on Jonah. He got so angry that he wanted to die. He cared more about his comfort than the lives of thousands of people. He played God; he judged that they should be shown no mercy. He didn't think of their suffering, just his own. He quoted from part of Exodus 34:6–7. He knew God was compassionate, but he was hoping God wouldn't be compassionate with Nineveh. Wow. How many times have I seen that in myself? I'm so worried about my own suffering or the threat of it that I couldn't care less about others' suffering. "I love that God is compassionate ... to me."

The book of Jonah ends with God saying,

> And he prayed unto the LORD, and said, I pray thee, O LORD, [was] not this my saying, when I was yet in my country? Therefore I fled before unto Tarshish: for I knew that thou [art] a gracious God, and merciful, slow to anger, and of great kindness, and repentest thee of the evil ... Then said the LORD, Thou hast had pity on the gourd, for the which thou hast not laboured, neither madest it grow; which came up in a night, and perished in a night: And should not I spare Nineveh, that great city, wherein are more than sixscore thousand persons that cannot discern between their right hand and their left hand; and [also] much cattle? (Jonah 4:2, 10–11)

The book of Jonah ends with that last sentence. God basically dropped the mic and walked away leaving Jonah with his mouth wide open. I wonder if some Christians have more compassion for their house plants than for their neighbors. It was sobering when I thought about all the trivial things I cared about growing up while at the same time lacking compassion for people. The second thing about God was rarely a blip on my radar.

Majoring in the minors was certainly something Christendom did during its darker times. They would kill someone just for saying the Lord's Prayer in English back in William Tyndale's day. You may look back at growing up in a church whose members majored in the minors too. If I could put my childhood memories of church in a nutshell, it would be getting saved and the return of Christ. In between were all the minors—having the proper haircut, clothes, etc.

Majoring in the minors certainly was a thing in Jesus's day. He said that they strained at a gnat as they swallowed a camel (Matthew 23:24b). They were worried about things such as giving one-tenth down to the bean. Jesus said that they "omitted the weightier matters of the law, judgment, mercy, and faith" (Matthew 23:23b).

When we hear the word *law*, it may drum up the thought of ridged rules, but the Old Testament Law is full of compassion and kindness—not accepting someone's coat for payment when it's cold, fair wages, paying people on time, returning people their rightful property, loving neighbors, and being kind to new folks in town, the poor, and animals. When Jesus was talking about the Law and justice, He was talking about these things.

There was a big problem with those things in Old Testament times. The powerful robbed the poor of justice and trumped up their own traditions to get out of being compassionate even to their aging parents. When Jesus talked of justice, He wasn't saying they needed to punish more people and be more strict about the Sabbath. In fact, He even stopped the stoning of the woman caught in adultery. He was saying that they needed to treat people rightly and fairly ... to actually care for people.

Let's take a look at Matthew 7:22–23.

Many will say to me in that day, Lord, Lord, have we not prophesied in thy name? and in thy name have cast out devils? and in thy name done many wonderful works? And then will I profess unto them, I never knew you: depart from me, ye that work iniquity.

These verses were at the end of the Sermon on the Mount (Matthew 5–7). Jesus was always warning His disciples and people about the way of the religious hard-liners of His day (Matthew 5:20). He started with the beatitudes—being humble, meek, and merciful peacemakers and living God's way even under persecution. He talked about being salt and light and the condition of the heart, not just keeping the letter of the Law. He spoke about loving enemies, doing things because they were right and out of a relationship with God, not for appearances' sake. So what was the lawlessness ("iniquity" in the KJV) of these religious people of whom Jesus said He never knew? The two biggies of the Law are loving God and loving people. The lawless are the religious fat cats of the day who totally did not practice these two things. They loved the flash ... they loved the power ... but they didn't love God and they didn't love people.

You can see justice, mercy, and faithfulness brought up often in similar situations in the Old Testament by prophets admonishing Israel and Judah and especially the corrupt and powerful to change and live by these things.

> Thus speaketh the LORD of hosts, saying, Execute true judgment, and shew mercy and compassions every man to his brother: And oppress not the widow, nor the fatherless, the stranger, nor the poor; and let none of you imagine evil against his brother in your heart. (Zechariah 7:9–10)

> He hath shewed thee, O man, what [is] good; and what doth the LORD require of thee, but to do justly, and to love mercy, and to walk humbly with thy God? (Micah 6:8)

> Therefore turn thou to thy God: keep mercy and judgment, and wait on thy God continually. (Hosea 12:6)

> Justice and judgment [are] the habitation of thy throne: mercy and truth shall go before thy face. (Psalm 89:14)

> Mercy and truth are met together; righteousness and peace have kissed [each other]. (Psalm 85:10)

I believe these are sorts of abbreviated versions of God's attributes found in Exodus 34:6–7 and mentioned elsewhere in the Bible pertaining to God and humans in relationship with God and each other.

- The realm of love—compassion, mercy, grace, kindness, patience, gentleness, forgiveness
- The realm of truth—faithfulness, trust, belief, faith
- The realm of righteousness—justice, judgment, goodness

In 1 Corinthians 13, the love chapter, is a concentration of things in the realm of love. These three realms intersect and support each other. When we realize and experience God's love, truth, and righteousness, we are drawn to humility and worship, and it results in peace and joy.

God created us and everything good, and He loves us. He is righteous, and He made a right way for everything to operate. There is a truth about the way things are meant to be. God is faithful to who He is and how He set things in order and to His Word and His relationship with us. There is a great peace and joy in that.

We can trust Him, believe His Word, have faith in His abilities, and do things the right way. We can return His love. Though we are fallen, He still loves us, has compassion for us, grants us mercy and grace, shows us kindness, and forgives us.

God corrects us like any good father would. He is righteous and has a standard; though He renders judgment and gives justice, He offers His righteousness in exchange for our unrighteousness made possible by His sacrifice of love.

Some might say, "But the Bible says we were given power and the ability to judge." Yes, God gave us power to act compassionately by healing, casting out demons, and other gifts of the Spirit, for overcoming our sinful nature, and living godly lives but not for controlling people. Only on rare occasions was apostolic power used differently such as blindness upon the sorcerer, Elymas, by Paul in Acts 13:6–12. Even so, the text makes it clear that it was brought on by the Holy Spirit because the false prophet was seeking to turn the deputy away from faith.

Controlling people is not God's power in humanity; it is humanity trying to have God's power. We realize we are flawed while God is not; we can surrender to the control of the Holy Spirit. Even then, the Holy Spirit is gentle and does not take control by force like an uninvited evil spirit.

Yes, we are given the ability to judge right now between right and wrong, true and false. There will always be matters that pop up in the church that will require us to judge between right and wrong such as 1 Corinthians 6.1–6. Paul said that the works of the sinful nature were obvious, so they don't require much judgment. The Bible is pretty clear on most things, and Paul pointed out that the least of us should be able to deal with trivial matters. Later, in our redeemed bodies, we will judge the world and angels (1 Corinthians 6:2–3), but now is not the time for that.

We should let God be God and not grasp for power; we should let God make His righteous judgments. We can trust that He judges right and that we should not take up the gavel ourselves. We should take to heart the compassion, mercy, love, kindness, and forgiveness He gives us and forward it to others.

CHAPTER 3

WHAT IS COMPASSION?

The word *compassion* comes from the Latin word *passions,* meaning "suffering." The prefix is *com,* "with." It takes on the meaning "to suffer with," to take on another's suffering. Empathy is a close synonym. When we have compassion for others, we feel and understand their suffering and are moved to take action. Rather than with a dictionary quote, I prefer to define biblical compassion from biblical usage.

Compassion Is God's Nature

In Exodus 34:6–7 KJV, "merciful," is translated "is compassionate" (*Strong's Hebrew Lexicon* H7349), and about half of the biblical versions translate it as "compassionate." I believe mercy and compassion are two sides of the same coin, but more on that later. *Strong's* H7349 is found thirteen times in the OT and is used only in reference to God. God has a pure, deep level of compassion no one can match, so that seems fitting.

God told Moses in Exodus 33:19a, "I will make all my goodness pass before thee, and I will proclaim the name of the LORD before thee." Exodus 34:6–7 was exactly what God said. One can make the argument that compassionate is part of the Lord's name like a title or who He is. Kings often did the same thing in ancient times. A king's name might include descriptive words such as "the merciful" or "protector." King Philip of England had 133 words to his official title at last count.

God is (Isaiah 6:5b) the King, the Lord of hosts; 1 Titus 1:17a reads, "Now unto the King eternal, immortal, invisible, the only wise God." Psalm 95:3 reads, "For the LORD [is] a great God, and a great King above all gods," and 1 Titus 6:15b reads, "... the King of kings, and Lord of lords." Psalm 29:10b reads, "King for ever," and Psalm 47:7a says, "God [is] the King of all the earth." Revelation 15:3b calls God the "King of saints." These are just a few descriptions of God's kingship; they have to do with God's awesome power and position. What I love about Exodus 34:6 is that it speaks centrally of God's character: "The LORD, The LORD God, merciful and gracious, longsuffering, and abundant in goodness and truth."

However, several Hebrew words can be translated "compassion"; they bring out its different aspects. *Chamal* (*Strong's* H2550) described Pharaoh's daughter when she found Moses in the basket: "And when she had opened [it], she saw the child: and, behold, the babe wept. And she had compassion on him, and said, This [is one] of the Hebrews' children" (Exodus 2:6). It has the sense of sparing someone; isn't that interesting? The thing Moses's sister was counting on, compassion, to save his life was the first thing God revealed about His heart to Moses some eighty years later.

God's compassion is compared to a father's compassion for his children: "Like as a father pitieth [his] children, [so] the LORD pitieth them that fear him" (Psalm 103:13). "Pitieth" in the KJV is *racham* (*Strong's* H7355; also translated "compassion"). One of my earliest memories was when I was barely old enough to stand. I was sick, and my father placed his hand on my head. Even a baby can feel the power of compassion.

My father and brother came to see me when I was a young man and had just learned that my wife was divorcing me. As I told them, there was no negative talk from them about my wife, no "I told you it wasn't a good idea," I saw the compassion in my brother's and father's eyes. My father put his hand on top of mine. It would be hard for anyone to match that level of compassion. My father had a great love for me. He was suffering because his son was suffering. It was as if some of my pain left me.

God's compassion is described as greater than the closest bond in nature—that of a mother and her baby. I couldn't begin to tell you how many times my mother had compassion on me as a child and did all she could to stop my suffering. Isaiah 49:15 reads, "Can a woman forget her sucking child, that she should not have compassion on the son of her womb? yea, they may forget, yet will I not forget thee." It is no wonder Paul called God the "Father of mercies" (2 Corinthians 1:3b; translated "compassion" elsewhere).

Just as it is natural for fathers and mothers to show compassionate to their children, it is God's divine nature to be compassionate to all His creation. "The LORD [is] gracious, and full of compassion; slow to anger, and of great mercy. The LORD [is] good to all: and his tender mercies [are] over all his works" (Psalm 145:8–9).

Compassion Is for the Innocent and the Guilty

Compassion is not only for the innocent, those who suffer through no fault of their own, but also for those who ended up in bad places because they did not listen to God, went their own way, and did something evil or foolish.

As soon as the Prodigal Son's father saw him returning humbly, he was filled with compassion. The father didn't put him down or chew him out. "And he arose, and came to his father. But when he was yet a great way off, his father saw him, and had compassion, and ran, and fell on his neck, and kissed him" (Luke 15:20).

The Bible points out that God was full of compassion even for those who had forsaken Him and had turned to other gods time after time. Nehemiah spoke about the history of Israel and Judah doing this starting when they had barely left captivity in Egypt to the exile to Babylon, about 1,000 years. Every time Israel forsook God, He had compassion on His people and did not forsake them.

Let's take a look at what Nehemiah said of Israel and God during this time from Nehemiah 9.

- Of Israel when they just left Egypt: "And refused to obey, neither were mindful of thy wonders that thou didst among them; but hardened their necks, and in their rebellion appointed a captain to return to their bondage" (v. 17a).
- Of God: "Thou [art] a God ready to pardon, gracious and merciful, slow to anger, and of great kindness, and forsookest them not" (v. 17b).
- Of Israel in the wilderness: "Yea, when they had made them a molten calf, and said, This [is] thy God that brought thee up out of Egypt, and had wrought great provocations" (v. 18).
- Of God: "Yet thou in thy manifold mercies forsookest them not in the wilderness" (v. 19).
- Of manifold mercies (many acts of compassion): "The pillar of the cloud departed not from them by day, to lead them in the way; neither the pillar of fire by night, to shew them light, and the way wherein they should go. Thou gavest also thy good spirit to instruct them, and withheldest not thy manna from their mouth, and gavest them water for their thirst. Yea, forty years didst thou sustain them in the wilderness, [so that] they lacked nothing; their clothes waxed not old, and their feet swelled not" (vv. 19b–21).
- Of Israel during the time of the judges when its people were in the Promised Land: "Nevertheless they were disobedient, and rebelled against thee, and cast thy law behind their backs, and slew thy prophets which testified against them to turn them to thee, and they wrought great provocations. Therefore thou deliveredst them into the hand of their

enemies, who vexed them: and in the time of their trouble" (vv. 26–27a).

- Of God: "When they cried unto thee, thou heardest [them] from heaven; and according to thy manifold mercies thou gavest them saviours, who saved them out of the hand of their enemies" (v. 27b).

- Of Israel in the time of the kings: "But after they had rest, they did evil again before thee: therefore leftest thou them in the hand of their enemies, so that they had the dominion over them" (v. 28a).

- Of God: "Yet when they returned, and cried unto thee, thou heardest [them] from heaven; and many times didst thou deliver them according to thy mercies" (v. 28b).

- Of Israel: "And testifiedst against them, that thou mightest bring them again unto thy law: yet they dealt proudly, and hearkened not unto thy commandments, but sinned against thy judgments, (which if a man do, he shall live in them;) and withdrew the shoulder, and hardened their neck, and would not hear" (v. 29).

- Of God: "Yet many years didst thou forbear them, and testifiedst against them by thy spirit in thy prophets: yet would they not give ear: therefore gavest thou them into the hand of the people of the lands. Nevertheless for thy great mercies' sake thou didst not utterly consume them, nor forsake them; for thou [art] a gracious and merciful God" (vv. 30–31).

It was amazing that no matter how many times Israel and Judah messed up, God had compassion on His problem children. Finally, they were at a place in Nehemiah's day after they returned from exile where they said, "Howbeit thou [art] just in all that is brought upon us; for thou hast done right, but we have done wickedly" (Nehemiah 9:33). That should give us hope. No wonder why Jeremiah could look at the smoldering remains of Jerusalem after a lost battle and still say, "This I recall to my mind, therefore have I hope. [It is of] the LORD'S mercies that we are not consumed, because his compassions fail not. [They are] new every morning: great [is] thy faithfulness" (Lamentations 3:21–23).

We are not faithful so many times, but God is always faithful … and compassionate.

Compassion Crosses Enemy Lines

It is amazing what can be done when compassion is put before politics: "He hath shewed thee, O man, what [is] good; and what doth the LORD require of thee, but to do justly, and to love mercy, and to walk humbly with thy God?" (Micah 6:8). I think the idea here is that we should focus on doing right, be merciful even when others are not doing right, and stay humble knowing we need God's mercy. The world says, "I want my justice and I want it now!" But what if we were to love mercy first? Paul said it was better to suffer a wrong than for two Christians to make a spectacle in court in front of the world in 1 Corinthians 6:6–7.

> But brother goeth to law with brother, and that before the unbelievers. Now therefore there is utterly a fault among you, because ye go to law one with another. Why do ye not rather take wrong? why do ye not rather [suffer yourselves to] be defrauded?

I was once in court for the emotional support of a friend who had a legitimate claim against a woman who had threatened her. Also in the court were several other people petitioning for restraining orders. One woman wanted a restraining order against a woman who had called her names to other church members behind her back. I couldn't believe this was in front of a judge. In James 2:13b, we read, "Mercy rejoiceth against judgment." In the Old Testament, the Law was in the ark of the covenant, but the mercy seat was over the law. In this case, two Christians could not find it in their hearts to put mercy above name-calling. The judge tried to keep a straight face and threw the request out quickly.

Earlier, we looked at how God sent Jonah to Nineveh, his nation's enemy, to show the Ninevites compassion. Jesus told a parable that had a couple of things in common with Jonah's lesson. In the story of the Good Samaritan, a priest and then a Levite, religious leaders, passed right by a man who had been beaten, robbed, and left half-dead. Maybe that sounds like some parts of town you know. It was an area between Jerusalem and Jericho, and the man who had been beaten was no doubt a Jew. Then it gets interesting. "But a certain Samaritan, as he journeyed, came where he was: and when he saw him, he had compassion [on him]" (Luke 10:33). The Samaritan took care of the man and got him to an inn.

Remember how God's lesson to Jonah was to be compassionate *toward* an enemy (Nineveh)? Well now, with the story of the Good Samaritan, Jesus was teaching them compassion by giving an example of when it came *from* the enemy. Samaritans were half Assyrian, and the Jews despised them. They wouldn't have eaten with this Samaritan, but he was the one who had compassion on a Jew when other Jews didn't. Looks like the compassion lesson has come full circle. Shouldn't we have compassion on enemies? Romans 5:10 makes it clear that we were all enemies of God but He had compassion on us.

Another interesting point—this story came up after Jesus talked with experts of the Levitical Law. One of the things brought up was loving neighbors as yourself. Someone asked whom his neighbors were. They were talking about love, but an example of compassion was given. It shows how important compassion is in the realm of love. Kindness and gentleness, also in the realm of love, can be seen by the Samaritan in the story as well.

Compassion Is the Start of Action

Why did I not focus on the third or fourth thing about God? Why didn't I make the focus grace, kindness, or forgiveness? It's because compassion seems to be a catalyst to action. If someone has compassion for someone, patience, mercy, kindness, forgiveness, and comfort follow right along. We can see how gentle, patient, and kind God was with Israel trying to get its people to repent for years and forgiving them when they repented. It starts with God's disposition to compassion, His eyes of compassion not only for Israel but going back to the fall. Adam and Eve sinned but were given hope, and God covered their shame. Their son, Abel, was murdered, but they were given another son, Seth. Even Cain was given a measure of comfort in protection from revenge. The ground was cursed, but Noah was given a gift to farm. With all suffering even from punishment comes a measure of compassion.

We can often see God's power to comfort after He had shown compassion. It's no wonder that right after Paul called Him the "Father of mercies" (2 Corinthians 1:3), he called Him "the God of all comfort." Grace is coupled with compassion in Exodus 34:6 and 33:19. Grace is something we receive from God, something we don't deserve or can earn. It is also strength to bear with suffering. In Paul's suffering, God gave him grace (2 Corinthians 12:7–9). Even when our suffering is deserved or for some reason necessary, God in His compassion provides grace that comes alongside it.

Compassion Has Hands of Mercy

The words *mercy* and *compassion* are used interchangeably in some verses of versions of the Bible. Here is something that may shed light on that. The blind men asked for mercy (Matthew 20:31): "And the multitude rebuked them, because they should hold their peace: but they cried the more, saying, Have mercy on us, O Lord,

[thou] Son of David." Jesus was then moved with compassion and granted them an act of mercy: "Jesus had compassion [on them], and touched their eyes: and immediately their eyes received sight, and they followed him" (Matthew 20:34).

Here is the same thing in Psalms 51:1, except David was asking for forgiveness of sin instead of restoration of sight: "Have mercy upon me, O God, according to thy lovingkindness: according unto the multitude of thy tender mercies blot out my transgressions" (Psalm 51:1). David asked for mercy, but where did he say it stemmed from? Because God has unfailing love and great compassion (tender mercies), David believed he could plead for mercy, which took the form of blotting out his transgressions. I see it like this: compassion is the egg that hatches an act of mercy.

Above, you have the expression of both words used in a single situation. However, I believe that many times in the Bible, the words *compassion* and *mercy* are used in situations where both occurred, but one is written and one is implied. I suppose someone could show mercy but really have no compassion, no thought to the pain of the one being shown mercy perhaps for some ulterior motive, but that isn't the case with God.

CHAPTER 4

JESUS: MASTER OF COMPASSION

Jesus is the exact representation of God (Hebrews 1:3) in the flesh (John 1:14), so it should not be surprising that because Exodus 34:6 says compassion is the first thing about God's character, we see it is the first thing about Jesus's character. If someone has problems believing in the divinity of Christ solely from the miracles He did, how about adding His character to the evidence?

Some people might not think God meant the things in Exodus 34:6–7 in any particular order. However, when we look at the ministry of Jesus, it's obvious that compassion came first. Even the start of Jesus's ministry was kicked off with a scripture all about compassion. Jesus quoted from Isaiah 61 in Luke 4:18–19 and blew their minds with the next two verses.

> The Spirit of the Lord [is] upon me, because he hath anointed me to preach the gospel to the poor; he hath sent me to heal the brokenhearted, to preach deliverance to the captives, and recovering of sight to the blind, to set at liberty them that are bruised, To preach the acceptable year of the Lord. And he closed the book, and he gave [it] again to the minister, and sat down. And the eyes of all them that were in the synagogue were fastened on him.

> And he began to say unto them, This day is this
> scripture fulfilled in your ears. (Luke 4:18–21)

And did He ever! He was anointed to do acts of compassion. Perhaps the best way He demonstrated compassion was in His ministry. The gospels record the many times Jesus was moved by compassion before He acted. He had compassion for the hungry before He fed them: "Have compassion on the multitude, because they have now been with me three days, and have nothing to eat" (Mark 8:2).

You know the story: Jesus fed 4,000 with seven loaves of bread and a few fish. In Matthew 14, Jesus fed well over 5,000 with only five loaves of bread. This act of compassion inspired many to feed the hungry even to this day.

Jesus was moved with compassion before He healed the sick: "And Jesus went forth, and saw a great multitude, and was moved with compassion toward them, and he healed their sick" (Matthew 14:14).

Can you imagine the disciples seeing this look of compassion come over Jesus's face as He looks out at the thousands of people? He saw how confused they were. He saw how burdened they were. He saw how weary they were. He saw how they suffered from so many things. Many had walked miles bringing their sick and calling out to Him. So He went into this sea of people healing the first sick person He saw ... and the next one ... then the next one. He moved through the multitude leaving a train of rejoicing behind Him and hope springing up ahead of Him.

Jesus had compassion on the blind before He healed them.

> And, behold, two blind men sitting by the way
> side, when they heard that Jesus passed by, cried
> out, saying, Have mercy on us, O Lord, [thou] Son
> of David. ... So Jesus had compassion [on them],
> and touched their eyes: and immediately their eyes

received sight, and they followed him. (Matthew
20:30, 34)

What I found interesting here was that people were telling them
to be quiet! "And the multitude rebuked them, because they should
hold their peace: but they cried the more, saying, Have mercy on us,
O Lord, [thou] Son of David" (Matthew 20:31). Hey! They were not
the blind ones! How can we be so blind to the sufferings of others
that we even try to stop them from reaching the one person who
can help? They were so embarrassed by a scene that they lacked all
compassion for the blind men.

Have you ever noticed that the people who are not suffering at
the moment can have a total lack of urgency to help those who are
suffering?. The blind guys were like, "Forget your feelings! I want my
sight back!" We should never let anyone's feelings (or I should say
lack of feelings or compassion) get between us and God. I'm with
the blind men: "Jesus, have mercy on me!"

Jesus Had Compassion for the Demon-Possessed Man

The man with a legion of demons in him was so strong and
violent that he would break his chains and fetters. People had to go
around and couldn't cross the shore on that side. He stayed in the
mountains and tombs; he was tormented and crying, and he would
cut himself. Jesus didn't go to the other side; He had compassion
for the man.

Jesus cast the demons out and left the man in his right mind:
"Howbeit Jesus suffered him not, but saith unto him, Go home to
thy friends, and tell them how great things the Lord hath done for
thee, and hath had compassion on thee" (Mark 5:19).

The man wanted to tag along with Jesus after that—and I can
understand wanting to—but Jesus knew he had friends and family
who needed to know about His compassion too. It is nice to bask in

the Lord's comfort, but others are suffering and need hope. Others need to know that God is compassionate, and when they see what God has done for us, they can be inspired to go the Lord as well.

Jesus Was Moved with Compassion for the Unclean

One very touching story was about a man who had leprosy, a horrible disease. People infected with it could lose their sense of touch and as a result were often covered in sores. They were considered unclean and had to stay away from others. They were shunned. They were lonely. They were waiting to die. Anyone who touched them would also be considered unclean. This broken man with leprosy knelt before Jesus and begged Him to make him clean: "And Jesus, moved with compassion, put forth [His] hand, and touched him, and saith unto him, I will; be thou clean" (Mark 1:41).

As amazing as the healing was, the way He did it was incredibly powerful. Jesus was moved with compassion; He knew and felt the pain the man was feeling due to his disease, his being shunned, and his having to bear the stigma of being unclean.

Notice that the man did not say, "Heal me." He said, "If thou wilt, thou canst make me clean" (Mark 1:40b). As a leper, everywhere the man went, he had to shout "Unclean! Unclean!" Jesus could have only spoken and the man would have been healed, but He did something no one dared do—He touched the man while he was still unclean. It wasn't until Jesus spoke that the man was healed. "And as soon as he had spoken, immediately the leprosy departed from him, and he was cleansed" (Mark 1:42).

I want everyone who is suffering because of a stigma or feeling that they are outcasts in any way to know that Jesus knows their pain. He knew that man's loneliness, He knew his rejection, He knew his self-loathing, and He knew his fear. I want to tell those who are suffering that they don't need to go get clean for Jesus because

He will put His hand of compassion on them and make them 100 percent clean, 100 percent acceptable in His sight.

Jesus Was Moved with Compassion before He Raised the Dead

A widow from a city called Nain was on her way to bury her only son. You can imagine her pain. She walked crying with a broken heart as she escorted her dead son to the cemetery. But someone saw her.

> And when the Lord saw her, he had compassion on her, and said unto her, Weep not. And he came and touched the bier: and they that bare [him] stood still. And he said, Young man, I say unto thee, Arise. And he that was dead sat up, and began to speak. And he delivered him to his mother. (Luke 7:13–15)

I remember an old joke about Jesus going to four funerals and ruining every one of them including His own. Jesus wept at Lazarus's tomb even knowing He was going to raise him from the dead in a matter of minutes. I believe that was out of sheer compassion for the pain Lazarus's family had experienced and on some level for the pain everyone had felt from death down through the ages. The Bible calls death an enemy of God. I can only imagine how God, the most compassionate being there is, felt seeing all the sorrow of death on all people from Adam to now.

As many times as I have heard and read about the healings of Jesus, I must admit to my shame that for most of my life, I barely if at all noticed the compassion before the power. I have been to church services in many different denominations. When it comes to healing, it seems that many focus on the faith of either the person being healed or the person asking God for the healing. I have seen a room full of people trying to drum up enough faith for a healing.

But rarely did Jesus ask people if they believed; He simply had compassion for them and healed them. Jesus of course knew He had the power; He had been the active element in the Creation and the active force holding all things together (Colossians 1:16–17). For Jesus, it was not a matter of faith but of compassion. Most knew Jesus had the power because they had seen or heard about it. If it was a matter compassion for Jesus, shouldn't our actions be a matter of compassion as well?

Jesus Did Not Let His Pain Get in the Way of His Compassion for Others

When John the Baptist was killed, Jesus went to a place to be alone and mourn. When a pet of mine died, I was full of pain and wanted to be alone as I buried him. I can only imagine the pain Jesus felt when His cousin, a humble man who had baptized Him, a man faithful to God, a man whom no man was greater than was murdered to please a dancing girl.

Jesus didn't let the sorrow in His heart consume Him to the point that He could not be compassionate to the needs of others: "And Jesus went forth, and saw a great multitude, and was moved with compassion toward them, and he healed their sick" (Matthew 14:14).

He got past the pain in His heart then, and He got past the pain in His heart and body on the cross. In all that excruciating pain He suffered on the cross, He forgave others and interceded for others; He made sure His mother had John as a son and John had His mother as a mother to comfort each other. In all that pain, He comforted a dying man with the promise of paradise.

How often do I let even slight irritations keep me from getting outside myself to the greater need of compassion for others. I am amazed at people who can get past the irritation caused by another person and actually help or comfort that person with a gentle spirit.

That quality is a must in the service industry. It takes a letting go and a putting on.

It's a win-win-win-win. Those who let go of their irritation and pain win because they are not holding that painful negativity inside any more. They also win because they are allowing the positive fruit of the Spirit to fill them with kindness, peace, gentleness, and goodness. They win because they know they are doing another human being good. Finally, they win because they will be rewarded in heaven. And let's not forget those who receive compassion and the effect it can have on them.

Here's an example of how even a minor situation of this quality can be impactful. I was with family at a nice restaurant for Mother's Day. The place had a great view of the woods from a glassed-in seating area. We decided to walk though that area to take in the view after our meal. Unfortunately, there was little room between tables, and as timing would have it, I found myself wedged in between a waiter and a table. That young man had every right to be irritated; there he was trying to do his job on a busy night in an already crowded area, and here comes some big guy into a place where he had no business being and getting in his way. With no guile, the young man turned to me and complimented me on my shirt. I felt like a new guy in town who had turned down a one-way street the wrong way and was helped out of the situation by someone coming the right way instead of being honked or yelled at.

CHAPTER 5

THE COMPASSION BLOCKER

If God has compassion on all His creation (Psalm 145:9), what can stop us from receiving it? Earlier, we learned that even after people have messed up time after time, God still showed them compassion. We saw it when Israel returned from exile, when the Ninevites humbled themselves, and when Prodigal Son returned. We saw compassion flow out of Christ to all who came to Him. It seems all we have to do to receive God's compassion is be humble enough to receive it. On the other hand, it seems the thing that can stifle the benefit of the first thing about God's nature is the first sin—pride. Pride is self-exaltation and self-absorption. It's hard to receive and show compassion if one is focused on one's self.

In King Hezekiah's day, there was a great revival in Judea. Just a few years earlier, the temple door had been shut by his wicked father, King Ahaz, and the land was overrun with idols. Hezekiah reopened the temple, got the priesthood in shape, and resumed sacrifice and worship. The people were full of joy.

However, the north was suffering. Israel had been invaded by Assyria because the Israelites had turned from God and ignored His many pleas through prophets to return to Him. Hezekiah reached out to Northern Israel in their suffings to receive God's compassion even though just a few years earlier, God had used them to destroy his father's army. Hezekiah reinstated the Passover and sent this invitation to Israel, which read in part,

> For if ye turn again unto the LORD, your brethren and your children [shall find] compassion before them that lead them captive, so that they shall come again into this land: for the LORD your God [is] gracious and merciful, and will not turn away [his] face from you, if ye return unto him. (2 Chronicles 30:9)

> Some unfortunately were too proud to receive it.

> So the posts passed from city to city through the country of Ephraim and Manasseh even unto Zebulun: but they laughed them to scorn, and mocked them. (2 Chronicles 30:10)

> Proud [and] haughty scorner [is] his name, who dealeth in proud wrath. (Proverbs 21:24)

> Nevertheless divers of Asher and Manasseh and of Zebulun humbled themselves, and came to Jerusalem. (2 Chronicles 30:11)

There was great joy and feasting during the Passover Feast. The revival continued to grow. God in His compassion reached out to those suffering, and those who responded were refreshed. How sad that so many missed out because of pride and remained in their suffering.

Another example was the time Jesus went back to His hometown: "And when he was come into his own country, he taught them in their synagogue, insomuch that they were astonished, and said, Whence hath this [man] this wisdom, and [these] mighty works?"

(Matthew 13:54). They were just too proud to humble themselves and believe the carpenter next door was the Messiah. They mocked Him: "Is not this the carpenter's son? is not his mother called Mary? and his brethren, James, and Joses, and Simon, and Judas?" (Matthew 13:55). Prideful people don't like to see the Joneses rising above them in any way. Apparently, it was a problem not just for Jesus but for many prophets in their home towns as well.

> And they were offended in him. But Jesus said unto them, A prophet is not without honour, save in his own country, and in his own house. And he did not many mighty works there because of their unbelief. (Matthew 13:57–58)

It wasn't that they didn't believe Jesus had wisdom and power; they had just said He did! It was because they refused to believe in spite of it and were even offended by that because they were too proud to honor Jesus; they could not place Him above themselves.

Have you ever seen people struggling with something but refusing all help? It wasn't because they didn't think others could help; it was because they were too proud to accept help. Maybe you can remember refusing help. I can, and pride was the only reason for it.

Someone once told me that right as he came out of a restaurant with a takeout sandwich, he saw a homeless man and had compassion for him. He offered the man his sandwich, and the man took it and threw it on the sidewalk saying, "I hate their food!"

Sadly, sometimes, the people who need compassion the most are those who reject it.

CHAPTER 6

LEARNING COMPASSION

But go ye and learn what [that] meaneth, I will have
mercy, and not sacrifice: for I am not come to call
the righteous, but sinners to repentance. (Matthew
9:13)

Jesus said this to the Pharisees because they were complaining
to His disciples about His eating with sinners. They didn't grasp
that ministry was a lot like doctors helping the sick. What good
are doctors if all they do is stand away from the patients, point,
and say, "You're sick!" You're sick? The Pharisees had read about
compassion in God's Word but obviously hadn't learned the lesson.
Head knowledge is one thing; experiential knowledge is another.

We can all learn to be more compassionate, but some children
of God are gifted in this area. The Greek word ἐλεῶν (*Strong's Greek
Lexicon* 1653) refers to a gift like teaching and prophecy: "Or he
that exhorteth, on exhortation: he that giveth, [let him do it] with
simplicity; he that ruleth, with diligence; he that sheweth mercy,
with cheerfulness" (Romans 12:8). Mostly translated "mercy" in
this verse, ἐλεῶν is translated "compassion" elsewhere. We looked
at how mercy and compassion go hand in hand. Apparently, even
those who have the gift of mercy are still being encouraged to use it
"with cheerfulness."

Sometimes, we are gifted to know what to do, but we still need to be mindful of how we do it. That goes for any spiritual gift. What if you had a waiter who knew to give you water and did but had a frown on his face and slammed it down? How often has a preacher preached 100 percent truth but in an angry or condescending way?

One reason Jesus suffered so much was to learn *manthano*, Greek translated as "experience," what we go through when we suffer. That made Him the perfect High Priest.

> Though he were a Son, yet learned he obedience by the things which he suffered; And being made perfect, he became the author of eternal salvation unto all them that obey him. (Hebrews 5:8–9)

It's not that Jesus had to learn obedience; it was that He experienced obedience while suffering so that He could empathize with us perfectly in our suffering to remain obedient.

Have your ever heard the phrase "Hurt people hurt people"? People who are hurting tend to lash out, don't they? All of a sudden, they start doing things that are very wrong because they are in pain. But even in all his pain, Jesus didn't lash out. Here was the most powerful person on earth in more pain than anyone else. If there was ever a time for someone to justifiably lash out due to pain, that would have been it. He had been betrayed, falsely accused, sentenced by a kangaroo court, beaten, whipped, mocked, and nailed to a cross for no crime. Instead of lashing out, He was compassionate. He thought about the pain of others. He was concerned for others and comforted them. He used His power to forgive the sins of the people killing Him and to grant eternal life to sinners—not to shoot out lightning bolts and call the armies of heaven to wipe them out.

Too many times, we hear about people in pain lashing out at others. Maybe they have some petty grievances. They are focused only on their own pain. They are not looking outward with a view of compassion, only inward to their pain. They play God, become as powerful as they can, and use that power to lash out and render judgment that is not at all righteous. That's the opposite of compassion. Compassion is feeling others' pain and using power to take away that pain. Too often, people force their pain on others. It's hard to show compassion when we are hurting, but Jesus did it, and He can help us do so as well.

Suffering Can Be a Way to Learn Compassion

One day, I woke up with a pain in my back. I thought it was an out-of-place vertebra or knotted-up muscle, but it just got worse. Soon, it felt like a dull knife was stuck in my upper back and my arm was on fire. Finally, I couldn't handle the pain and went to the hospital. The scans revealed I had a herniated disc. I could clearly see on the X-ray the herniation going out into the area of the spinal cord. A procedure stopped the pain.

I could have read about how painful a herniated disc could be, but it wasn't until it happened to me that I could truly understand the pain someone with the same condition could feel and be more compassionate toward them.

> Blessed [be] God, even the Father of our Lord Jesus Christ, the Father of mercies, and the God of all comfort; Who comforteth us in all our tribulation, that we may be able to comfort them which are in any trouble, by the comfort wherewith we ourselves are comforted of God. (2 Corinthians 1:3–4)

Job was one of the greatest of all men in the East. He was a godly man you couldn't point a finger at for anything. But oh, they tried! False accusations from his friends were added to his suffering along with the loss of his children, property, and health. Not to mention a wife who said his breath stank and that he should curse God and die.

> Behold, we count them happy which endure. Ye
> have heard of the patience of Job, and have seen the
> end of the Lord; that the Lord is very pitiful, and of
> tender mercy. (James 5:11)

However great Job was, he became greater because he experienced pain and then God's compassion for that pain. He became even more compassionate and comforting toward others having had that experience. We can use our suffering as well to gain knowledge of how to comfort others rather than just waste the opportunity to do that. One thing about suffering is that it will be over for those who put their faith in Christ.

We can have compassion for someone's suffering due to our having suffered as well, but we can also learn it when someone shows us compassion when we are suffering. Can you remember a time when someone relieved your suffering in some way and the impact that had on you? In the story of Job and in 2 Corinthians 1:3–4, we learn that God was compassionate; people can learn to be compassionate from what God did to them.

Unfortunately, not everyone learns from being shown compassion. Jesus told a story in Matthew 18:21–35 about someone who owed a ton of money to his lord. He begged the lord to have patience with him, and the lord had compassion on him and canceled his debt. Then that same man found a man who owed him little. He grabbed him by the neck and demanded what he owed. The man begged him to have patience just as he had asked his lord earlier. But the man would not and threw him in prison. When the man's lord found out about that, he said, "Shouldest not thou also have had compassion on thy fellowservant, even as I had pity on thee?" (Matthew 18:33).

It didn't go well for the servant who didn't learn compassion from the compassion shown to him. I hate to say it, but sometimes, a story of someone being very cruel can inspire us to be the opposite when we have empathy for the person suffering.

We learn compassion when we see it given to someone else. The story of the Good Samaritan, the Prodigal Son, and the many things Jesus did are inspiring. It can be contagious when we witness a powerful act of compassion whether live, on the news, or in a movie. When we are compassionate, we do the right thing and we inspire others.

CHAPTER 7

MAKING A DIFFERENCE

In Matthew 9:35–38, Jesus saw all these people and had compassion on them; He expressed to His disciples how much work there was to be done and how few people there were to do it. He asked them to pray that God would send more workers. As it turned out, they would be some of those workers. Right after that (Matthew 10), Jesus gave them power and sent them out to do all the things He had been doing when He had been moved with compassion (casting out demons and healing people).

It's great when a person with a billion dollars feels compassion for the poor and wants to reach out and help. It's even better when a billion people feel compassion and reach out and help. At the end of the day, it's not just some rich guy who will be held up to the light to see just how he did in being the number one way God is; it's all of us.

> Then shall the King say unto them on his right hand, Come, ye blessed of my Father, inherit the kingdom prepared for you from the foundation of the world: For I was an hungred, and ye gave me meat: I was thirsty, and ye gave me drink: I was a stranger, and ye took me in: Naked, and ye clothed me: I was sick, and ye visited me: I was in prison, and ye came unto me. (Matthew 25:34–36)

At the beginning of this book, there was no mistake about it; God was on the mountaintop with a massive display of power. Here, He was saying that He was the hungry, the thirsty, the stranger, the naked, the sick, the imprisoned ... What will we do when the power is in our hands? Will we be compassionate? Gracious? Patient? Kind? Forgiving?

You can see the contrast between Matthew 7:22–23 (those who based their salvation on their prophecy and power) and Matthew 25:34–36 (the compassionate the King welcomed). It's not a person's position (as a prophet or a preacher) or power (performing miracles or casting out demons) that guarantees a relationship with God. Wow! These are some remarkable and zealous things! If you recall, many will try to bring that up on the day of judgment but to no avail. Jesus seemed to be saying that the people who acted with God's heart of compassion were the ones who knew Him. If we walk with God, shouldn't we get to know His heart?

These are all acts of compassion, and they are not all big things. Even giving a cup of water. Sometimes, I get this crazy idea that I have to become successful so I can start this great foundation and help a lot of people. That's all great, but how many people would I pass up getting there who could have used just a cup of water, a bite to eat, a little company, or a little help with the rent? What if a lot of people did a little instead of a few doing a lot? If Christians do not show that they care about the suffering of others on Earth then how will people get the idea that they care if they suffer in eternity?

And of some have compassion, making a difference. (Jude 1:22)

Compassion always makes a difference even if it's just that cup of water. When God moves our hearts, it's for a reason, and it could make the difference in others' lives that leads them to the Father of compassion. And oh, the things that can change if we make a few small changes. Imagine the evil that would never happen and the good that would happen— far more than we could imagine.

And to know the love of Christ, which passeth knowledge, that ye might be filled with all the fulness of God. Now unto him that is able to do exceeding abundantly above all that we ask or think, according to the power that worketh in us, Unto him [be] glory in the church by Christ Jesus throughout all ages, world without end. Amen. (Ephesians 3:19–21)

A Prayer

Lord, I praise You, a God of compassion. I thank You for all the compassion You have had not only for me but also for the world. I know You suffered greatly on the cross in my place. I am sorry for all the suffering my sins have caused. I know that You know about all the ways I suffer, and I know You have comforted me and will continue to comfort me. Now, help me show Your compassionate heart to others in whatever way is Your will. Please show me how I can make a difference.

In Jesus's name I pray, amen.

ABOUT THE AUTHOR

Eleeo Zamzummin has been a student of scripture for 25 years and has spent over two decades in prison ministry. He has served as a layman preacher for First Christian Church in San Francisco since 2015.

His teaching, preaching and writing focus on the divine nature in the heart of God to inspire his audience to be greater participants of God's divine nature.

About the cover:

Cover art is by Sgt. Daniel G. Brewer (retrd). A veteran of two wars, Daniel was severely injured when a malfunctioning freight elevator door came down on his head in a V.A. hospital. Drawing became part of his therapy. He drew this cover to illustrate how even in Christ's suffering He was still holding the world together and in its place.

Printed in the United States
By Bookmasters